PIANO · VOCAL · GUITAR

# THE ORIGIN OF LOV[...] KA






ISBN 978-1-4768-9963-3

HAL•LEONARD®
CORPORATION
7777 W. BLUEMOUND RD. P.O. BOX 13819 MILWAUKEE, WI 53213

In Australia Contact:
**Hal Leonard Australia Pty. Ltd.**
4 Lentara Court
Cheltenham, Victoria, 3192 Australia
Email: ausadmin@halleonard.com.au





Visit Hal Leonard Online at
**www.halleonard.com**

# ORIGIN OF LOVE

Words and Music by MIKA,
NICHOLAS LITTLEMORE and PAUL STEELE

Moderately fast
C Csus2 C Csus C Csus2 C Csus
mf
C Csus2
Love is a drug and you are my cig - a - rette.
C Csus2 C
Love is ad - dic - tion, and you are my Nic - o - rette. Love is a drug, like choc -
Csus2 C Csus2
- 'late, like cig - a - rettes. I'm feel - ing sick; I've got to med - i - cate my - self.

C F/C C Csus2 C Csus2 C F/C
C Csus2 C/B
I want your love; don't try and stop me.
C Csus2 C
Can't get e-nough; still hang-ing off me. Your guilt-y heart,
don't let it break you. And if you pray, well, no one's gon-na save you.

C
G
Am7
Like ev - 'ry - one that you fear and ev - 'ry - thing you hold dear, e - ven the book in your pock -
F
Am7
Fsus2
- et, you are the sun and the light; you are the free-dom I fight.
G7sus
C
God will do noth-ing to stop it. The or - i - gin is you.
G
Am7
Fmaj7
You're the or - i - gin of

C G Am7 F
love.
C Csus2 G/B C
Love is a drug and you are my cig - a - rette. Love is ad - dic - tion and
C/D G/D C C/B
you are my Nic - o - rette. Love is a drug, like choc - 'late, like cig - a - rettes.
C
I'm feel - ing sick; I've got to med - i - cate my - self. Well, if God is a priest
3fr

G7
Am7
F
and the dev - il a slut, well, that's a rea - son for noth - ing.
Am7
Fsus2
Like ev - 'ry word that you preach, like ev - 'ry word that you teach,
Dm7
G7(add4)
with ev - 'ry rule that you breach, you know the or - i - gin is
C
G
you.
you. From the air I breathe to the love I need,

Am7
F
(You're the or - i - gin of
on - ly thing I know, you're the or - i - gin of
C
G
love.)
love. From the God a - bove to the one I love,
Am7
F
(The or - i - gin is
on - ly thing that's true: the or - i - gin is
C
G
you.)
you. From the air I breathe to the love I lead,

Am7
F
(You're the or - i - gin of
on - ly thing I know you're the or - i - gin of
C
G
love.)
love. From God a - bove to the one I love,
Am7
F
To Coda
on - ly thing that's true: that the or - i - gin is
C
F6
(Ma - dre de - us, de - us ma - chis - mo.
you.

C
F
Ma - dre de - us, de - us ma - chis - mo.
Dm7
G
Di - o de ma - dre de - us ma - chis - mo.
Dm7
G
Ma - dre de - us san - to spi - ri - to.
C
G7
Like stu - pid A - dam and Eve, they found their love in a tree,

Am7
F
God did - n't think they de - served it.
Am7
Fsus2
He taught them hate, taught them pride, gave them a leaf, made them hide.
Dm7
F/A
G/D
D.S. al Coda
Let's push their sto - ry a - side. You know the or - i - gin is
CODA
C6/9
G6
Am7
you.

F6/9
C
Some love's a pill and some
G
love is a can - dy cane.
Am7
It tastes so sweet, but leaves
F(add2)
you feel - ing sick with pain.
C
Your love is air; I breathe
G
it in a - round me.
Dm11
3fr
Don't know it's there, but with -

F6
Dm7
C/G
G
-out it I'm drown-ing.
Love.
Am7
Fmaj9
C
You're the or-i-gin of
love.
G
Am7
F(add2)
C
Love.
G
Am
F6/9
Eh-oh-eh-oh-ah.
You're the or-i-gin of

C
G(add4)
love, love, love, love, love. You're the or - i - gin of
Thank God that you found me.
Am7
F6/9
love, love, love, love, love. You're the or - i - gin of
Thank God that you found me.
C
G(add4)
love, love, love, love, love. You're the or - i - gin of
Thank God that you found me.
Am7
F6/9
love, love, love, love, love. You're the or - i - gin of
Thank God that you found me.

C
G(add4)
love, love, love, love, love. You're the or - i - gin of
Thank God that you found me.
Am7
F6/9
G/F
G7/D
love, love, love, love, love. You're the or - i - gin of
Thank God that you found me.
C
G(add4)
love.
Thank God that you found me.
Am7
F6/9
G/F
G/D
C
Thank God that you found me.

# LOLA

Words and Music by MIKA, JODI MARR
and BENJAMIN JAMES HENRY JACK GARRETT

Moderately fast
F C F C Am7 G F C
*
mp
Dm7 C Dm7 C Am7 G F C
Dm7 C Dm7 C
Peo - ple al - ways make me cra - zy, love me lots, don't love me may - be.
Sex - y lies and mys - ter - y, they don't bring out the best in me; keep
Why pre - tend to be so jad - ed? It's so eas - y just to hate it.
Am7 G F C
What's the point of sing - ing sil - ly love songs?
jump - ing from a lov - er to a - noth - er.
An - y - one can love you for a dol - lar.

* *Recorded a half step lower.*

Dm7
C
Dm7
C
Who they think they ag - i - tate? It's make me sad or make me jeal - ous.
Thank you for the time you've tak - en, clean - ing up the mess I'm mak - ing.
When you find your love's for real, you'll beg and bor - row, cheat and steal,
1
Am7
G
F
C
Dm7
C
Don't be - lieve a word, 'cause they are so wrong. Lo - la,
Dm7
C
Am7
G
F
C
Lo - la.
2, 3
Am7
G
F
C
Make the same mis - take o - ver and o - ver.
try'n' to get the mon - ey just to call her.

F C F C Am G
Lo - la, I've made up my mind. I'm not gon - na fall in
F C F C F C
love this time. Lo - la, I've made up my mind.
Am G To Coda F C Dm7 C
I'm not gon - na fall in love this time.
Dm7 C Am7 G F C
Lo - la.
D.S. al Coda
(take 3rd ending)

CODA
F
C
F
love this time.
Am
Em
Like a fish out of wa - ter, it picks you up
Am
and spits you out. Why do we e - ven both - er
Em
F
when there's on - ly one way out, and we both know it, lov - er.

Dm7 C Dm7 C Am7 G
Lo - la, I've made up my mind. I'm not gon - na fall in
1 F C 2 F C Dm7 C
love this time. love this time. And you can't stop it if you try. Love
Dm7 C Am7 G 1 F C
makes you laugh, love makes you cry. The old - est game in his - to - ry re - peat - ed. Well,
2 F C Dm7 C Dm7 C
peat - ed. Lo - la,

Am7 G F C Dm7 C
Lo - la, babe, it's just an - oth - er love song.
Lo - la, I've
Dm7 C Am7 G
made up my mind.
Lo - la, babe, it's just an - oth - er
1
F C
love song.
2
F C Dm7 C Dm7 C
love song. Ooh, ah, ooh,
Ah,
Repeat and Fade
Am7 G F C
ah. Ooh,
ah, oh.
Optional Ending
Am7 G F C
ah.
ah, oh.

# STARDUST

Words and Music by MIKA,
WAYNE HECTOR, ALESSANDRO BENASSI
and MARCO BENASSI

Moderately fast
C
F
Am7
mf
G7sus
C
F
I could be star - ing at some-bod - y new, __ but stuck in my head __
Am7
G7sus
C
__ is a pic-ture of you. __ You were the thun - der, I was the rain. __
F
Am7
G7sus
__ I wan-na know __ if I'll see you a - gain. __ I said I love __

* *Recorded a half step lower.*

C
F
Am7
you, and you said good-bye.
Ev-'ry-thing chang-es in the blink of an eye.
G7sus
C
F
It's been a while; I still car-ry the flame.
I wan-na know,
Am7
G7sus
C
will I see you a-gain?
See you a-gain,
F
Am7
Gsus
3fr
G
see you a-gain.
on the floor.
Want you to know
I want you to know

C
F
Am7
what you mean to me,
what will it take,
take you to see.
G7sus
G7
C
F
I could put a lit - tle
star - dust
in your
eyes,
put a lit - tle
Am7
G7sus
G7
C
sun - shine in your life.
Give me a lit - tle
hug, you'll feel the same.
To Coda
F
Am7
G7sus
G7
And I wan - na know,
will I see you a - gain?
I'll see you a - gain.
I feel like a fool,

C
F
'cause you're not e - ven there.
I'm writ - ing this song
Am7
G7sus
G7
and you don't e - ven care.
Throw me a life -
C
F
- line, o - pen the door,
I'll pick up my heart
Am7
G7sus
G7
D.S. al Coda
that you left on the floor.
On the floor,

CODA
G7sus
G7
C
Run - ning out of time that's rush - ing ___ by, ___
___ Will I see you a - gain? ___
F
Am7
G7sus
G7
___ and all the lit - tle things that make me ___ high. ___ But e - ven af - ter
C
F
Am7
all, what did I ___ do? ___ There's a lit-tle bit of me ___ and a lit-tle bit of you. _
G7(add4)
F
G(add4)
___ When will I see you a - gain? ___ When will I see you a - gain? _

Am7
C
F
When will I see you a - gain?
G
Am7
G7(add4)
When will I see you a - gain?
I could put a lit - tle
C
F
Am7
star - dust in your eyes,
put a lit - tle sun - shine in your life.
G7sus
C
F
Give me a lit - tle hug, you'll feel the same.
And I wan - na know,

Am7
G7sus
will I see you a - gain?
I could put a lit - tle
Will I see you a - gain?
C
F
Am7
star - dust in your eyes,
put a lit - tle sun - shine in your life.
G7sus
G7
C
F
Give me a lit - tle hug, you'll feel the same.
And I wan - na know,
Am7
G7sus
G7
Am7
Run - ning out of time that's rush - ing by,
will I see you a - gain,
will I see you a - gain?

F
C
G7sus
G7
and all the lit - tle things that make me high. But e - ven af - ter
Am7
F
C
all what did I do? There's a lit - tle bit of me and a lit - tle bit of you.
G7
C
F
When will I see you a - gain? When will I see you a - gain?
Am7
G7sus
N.C.
When will I see you a - gain?

# MAKE YOU HAPPY

Words and Music by MIKA, JODI MARR
and BENJAMIN JAMES HENRY JACK GARRETT

Moderately
N.C.
All I wan - na do is make_ you hap - py. All I wan - na do is make_
f
_ you hap - py. All I wan - na do is make_ you hap - py.
B♭
Dm
All I wan - na do is make_ you hap - py. All I wan - na do is make_

A♭maj7
E♭maj7
you hap - py. All I wan - na do is make you hap - py.
B♭
Fm
A♭
All these years of try - ing. If I said I'm hap - py,
E♭
B♭
Fm
I'd be ly - ing. Think it's love we're mak - ing, but if
A♭
E♭
B♭
Fm7/E♭
this is love, then watch me die on you.

A♭ E♭ B♭ Fm
4fr 3fr
May - be you can't hear me, but I
A♭ E♭ B♭
4fr 3fr
feel like scream - ing when you're near me. Save me from your
Fm A♭ E♭
4fr 3fr
theo - ries, at the ver - y least, just let me cry on you.
B♭ Fm7 A♭ E♭
4fr 3fr
Un - der - val - ued, love is a bolt from the blue.

B♭
Fm7
A♭
4fr
If on - ly you knew, but you were so
E♭
3fr
B♭
far from the truth. All I wan - na do is make _ you hap -
Dm
A♭maj7
- py. All I wan - na do is make _ you hap - py. All I wan - na
E♭maj7
3fr
B♭
do is make _ you hap - py. All I wan - na do is make _ you hap -

Dm
A♭maj7
- py. All I wan - na do is make ___ you hap - py. All I wan - na
E♭maj7
3fr
B♭
Fm
do is make ___ you hap - py. A heart's a ___ lone - ly hunt - er. We can't
A♭
4fr
E♭
3fr
B♭
fight the ___ cold ___ and fight the ___ hun - ger. Who can ___ you ___ re -
Fm
A♭
4fr
E♭
3fr
ly on? Can we share the ___ shoul - der that you ___ cry on?

B♭ Fm A♭ E♭
You
B♭ Fm A♭
talk; how can I lis - ten when I hear the peo - ple scream, tell - ing me the
E♭ B♭ Fm
things I should be - lieve in? I'll show you what I'm made of. They can't
A♭ E♭
cov - er up for me, 'cause they know there's noth - ing I'm a - fraid of.
4fr
3fr

Bb
Fm7
Ab
4fr
Eb
3fr
Un - der - val - ued, love is a bolt from the blue.
Bb
Fm7
Ab
4fr
Eb
3fr
If on - ly you knew, but you were so far from the truth.
Bb
Dm
All I wan - na do is make_ you hap - py. All I wan - na do is make_
Abmaj7
Ebmaj7
3fr
_ you hap - py. All I wan - na do is make_ you hap - py.

B♭
Dm
A♭
E♭
Nev-er gon-na
B♭
Dm
give you up. Nev - er gon - na sort you out. Where's it gon - na
A♭
E♭
get ya? I'm nev - er gon - na let you down. Nev - er gon - na
B♭
Dm
give you up. Nev - er gon - na sort you out. Where's it gon - na
4fr
3fr

A♭
1
E♭
get ya? I'm nev - er gon - na let you down. Nev - er gon - na
2
E♭
B♭
let you down. All I wan - na do is make _ you hap -
Dm
A♭maj7
- py. All I wan - na do is make _ you hap - py. All I wan - na
1
E♭maj7
B♭
do is make _ you hap - py. All I wan - na do is make _ you hap -

Dm
A♭maj7
- py. All I wan - na do is make you hap - py. All I wan - na
E♭maj7
2
E♭maj7
3fr
do is make you hap - py.
do is make you hap - py.
B♭/D
Dm/F
All I wan - na do is make you hap - py. All I wan - na do is make
A♭maj7
E♭maj7
you hap - py. All I wan - na do is make you hap - py.

# UNDERWATER

Words and Music by MIKA,
NICHOLAS LITTLEMORE and PAUL STEELE

Moderately
Dm
F
mf
C
Am7
Dm
Burst - ing
Fly - ing
F
through a blood - red sky, a
through a bright blue sky with a

C
Am7
slow land - slide, and the world I've left
space - boy high from the world I left
Dm
be - hind. It's e - nough to lose
be - hind. It's e - nough to lose
F
C
your head, dis - ap - pear
my head, dis - ap - pear
Am7
and not re - turn a - gain.
and not re - turn a - gain.

F
Csus
3fr
When I fall to my feet, wear - ing my
C
Am
heart on my sleeve, all I see just don't make
Dm
C/E
F
sense. You are the port of my call;
Csus
3fr
C
Am
you shot and leav - in' me raw, now I

Dm
know you're a - maz - ing. 'Cause
C F C Dm
all I need is the love you breathe.
C F
Put your lips on me and I can live
Am
un - der - wa - ter, un - der - wa - ter, un - der - wa -

Dm
Dm/A
B♭
B♭/F
ter,
F
F/C
Csus
3fr
C
un - der - wa -
1
Dm
Dm/A
B♭
B♭/F
ter.
F
F/C
Csus
3fr
C

2
Dm
Dm/A
B♭
Un - der - wa - ter, un - der - wa - ter. I can live
- ter.
B♭/F
F
F/C
un - der - wa - ter. With your love, I can breathe,
Csus
3fr
C
Dm
I can breathe un - der - wa - ter. Un - der - wa -

Dm/A
Bb
Bb/F
- ter, un - der - wa - ter. I can live un - der - wa -
F
F/C
C
- ter. With your love, I can breathe, I can breathe
Dm
Dm/E
Dm/F
un - der - wa - ter. Un - der - wa - ter, un - der - wa -
un - der - wa - ter.

B♭
B♭/F
F
- ter. {I / We} can live un - der - wa - ter. With your
F/C
1
C
love, {I can breathe, / we could breathe,} I can breathe un - der - wa -
Un - der - wa -
2
C
N.C.
we could breathe un - der - wa - ter.

# OVERRATED

Words and Music by MIKA
and JODI MARR

Moderately
G5
*
f
Gsus
G
Words get bro - ken,
Breathe out, breathe in;
Stars are ma - gic;
cut me o - pen.
throw me, liv - ing,
light this tra - gic
Em
Love con -
off the
crime of
found me, kill me quick - ly.
deep end while I'm
pas - sion. I'm just
Asus2
1
D5

* *Recorded a half step lower.*

2,3
D5
5fr
G
sleep - ing.
ask - ing.
I'm a craz - y fool;
Of-fered up my wrist
I'm a fool, ad - dict - ed
and you thought you hit it,
to the touch of you,
but your ar - row missed;
Em
to your poi - son kiss - es.
could-n't kill me with it.
What you got to lose?
All I asked of you
Am
What do you think this is?
was to free my pain
Noth-ing left to prove,
so you could - n't do

To Coda
Dsus
G
D
and we know that love is o - ver - rat - ed,
this to me a - gain.
Em
Bm
C/G
D/A
o - ver - rat - ed in this god - damn world.
G
D/G
Em/G
Bm/G
C/G
O - ver - rat - ed, o - ver - rat - ed in
D5
5fr
G
D
Em
Bm
this god - damn world. O - ver - rat - ed, o - ver - rat - ed,

C
D5
5fr
G
D
o - ver - rat - ed in ___ this god - damn world. O - ver - rat - ed,
Em
Bm
C
o - ver - rat - ed, o - ver - rat - ed in ___
D5
5fr
Em
D.S. al Coda
(take 3rd ending)
___ this god - damn world. ___
CODA
G
D/A
Em
Bm
C/G
O - ver - rat - ed, o - ver - rat - ed,

D/A
G
D/G
o - ver - rat - ed,
Em/G
Bm/G
C/G
o - ver - rat - ed in
D5
5fr
G
D
this god - damn world.
O - ver - rat - ed,
(Words get
Em
Bm
C
o - ver - rat - ed,
o - ver - rat - ed in
bro - ken,
cut me

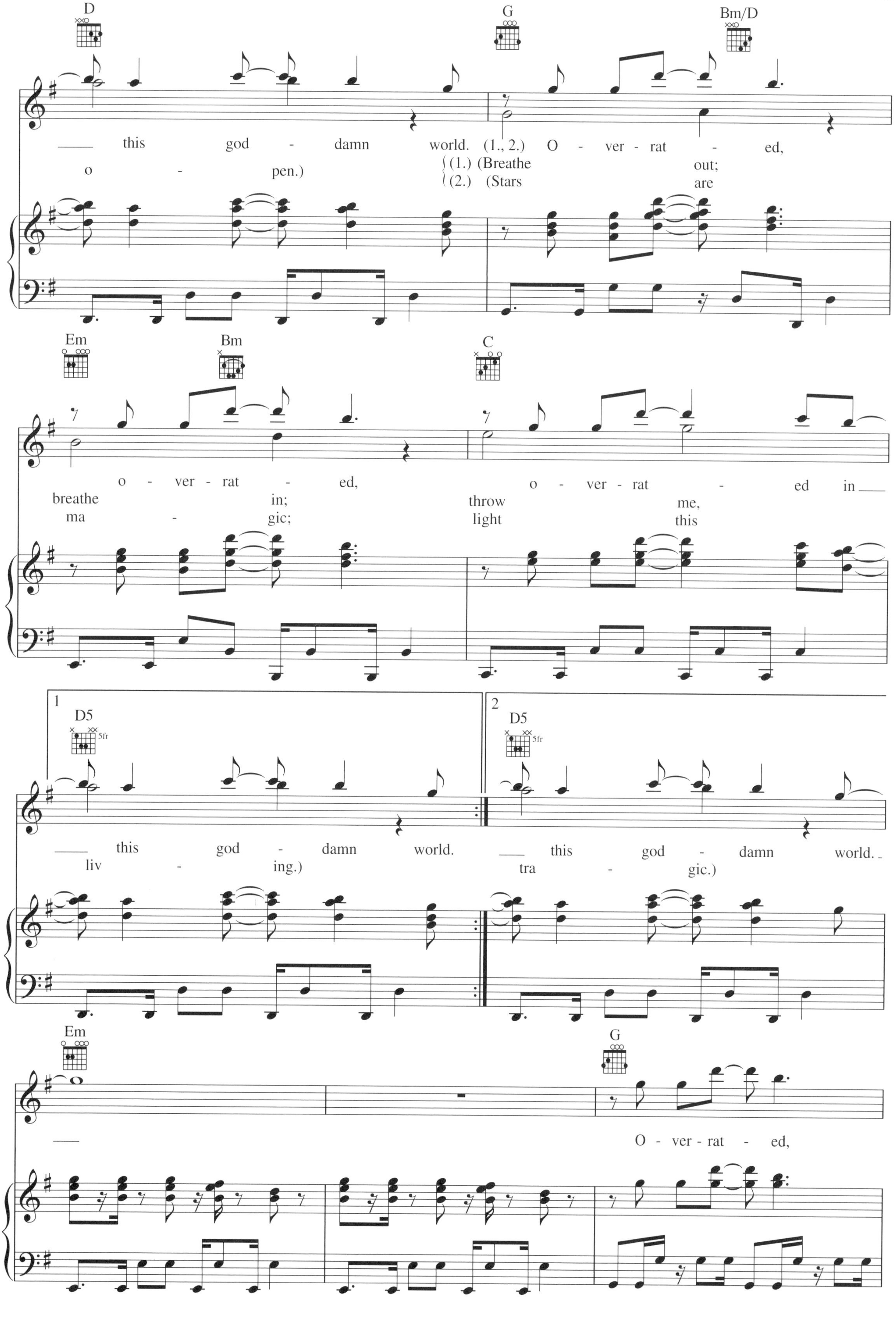
D
G
Bm/D
this god - damn world. (1., 2.) O - ver - rat - ed,
o - pen.) (1.) (Breathe out;
(2.) (Stars are
Em
Bm
C
o - ver - rat - ed, o - ver - rat - ed in
breathe in; throw me,
ma - gic; light this
1
D5
5fr
this god - damn world.
liv - ing.)
2
D5
5fr
this god - damn world.
tra - gic.)
Em
G
O - ver - rat - ed,

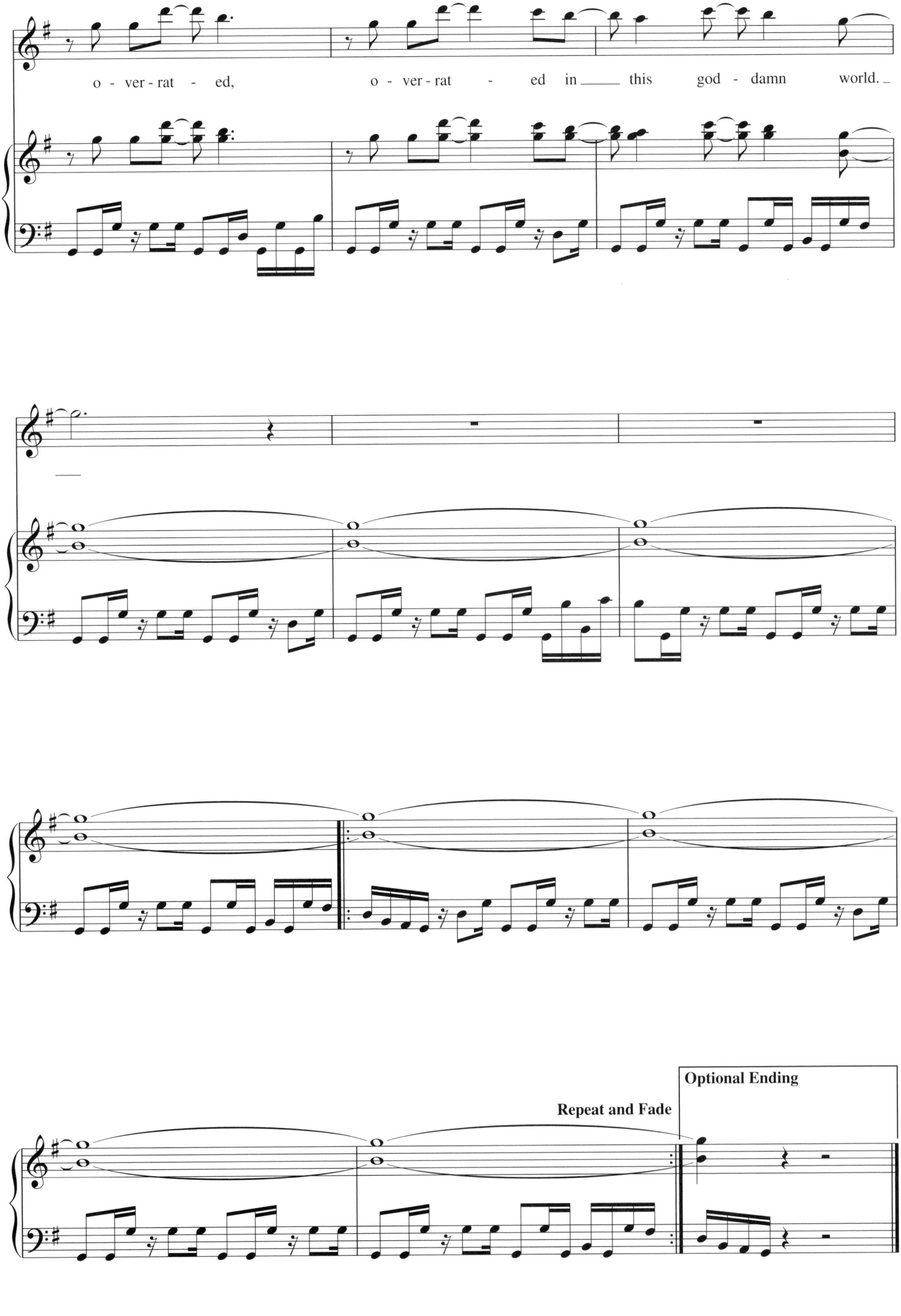
o - ver - rat - ed,
o - ver - rat - ed in this god - damn world.
Repeat and Fade
Optional Ending

# KIDS

Words and Music by MIKA
and NICHOLAS LITTLEMORE

Moderately
Dm7
mf
Gm
3fr
B♭(add2)
3fr
C
Dm
The
kids are play - ing in the sun.
They think their life has just be - gun.

Gm
B♭
For them it's just an - oth - er day, playing
C
Dm
games on - ly kids would play. There won't be a me and you
Gm
if we keep on fight - ing like we do.
B♭
C
Ba - by, don't you walk a - way, say - ing things on - ly kids would say.
3fr

F
E♭
3fr
B♭sus2
Kids, what do they know 'bout noth - in' at all?
Csus2
3fr
F
E♭
3fr
Lov - er, love when you're here and I love
B♭sus2
C7
F(add2)
when you're gone. Just an - oth - er Cal - i - for - nia day. Take your
kid gloves off. This is love, not war.

Dm
B♭(add2)
3fr
Give our peace a chance; make it worth
C7
F
fight - ing for. Take your kid gloves off.
Dm
This is love, not war. Give our
B♭(add2)
3fr
C
peace a chance; make it worth fight - ing for.

Dm
Gm7
B♭
C
Dm
You
You're
shout with noth - ing to say,
play - ing in the sand and sun;
and
you

Gm
fight 'til you get your way.
think your life has just be - gun.
It
You're
B♭
hurts, but what can I do?
throw - ing all my love a - way.
I won't
Just an -
C
F
E♭
turn in - to a kid too.
oth - er Cal - i - for - nia day.
Kids, what do they know 'bout noth -
Kids, what do they know 'bout noth -
B♭sus2
C7sus
F
- in' at all?
- in' at all? Just an - oth - er Cal - i - for - nia day.
Lov - er,

E♭
B♭sus2
love when you're here and I love when you're gone.
Just an -
C7
F(add2)
oth - er Cal - i - for - nia day.
Take your kid gloves off.
This is love, not war.
Dm
Give our
peace a chance;
B♭(add2)
make it worth
C7
fight - ing for.

F
Take your kid gloves off. This is
love, not war.
Dm
Give our peace a chance;
B♭(add2)
3fr
make it worth
C
fight - ing for.
N.C.

# LOVE YOU WHEN I'M DRUNK

Words and Music by MIKA
and JODI MARR

Moderately fast
G7(add4)
C
F
*f*
Dm
Gsus
G
C
F
I had a dream last night I slept with some - one else.
Dm
Gsus
G
C
Does that mean that I cheat - ed on you?
It was a - maz - ing, and I

F Dm Gsus 3fr G C
could-n't stop my-self. Could it be that I real-ly want to?
C/E F
When if the things we feel count more than what we do,
Dm Gsus 3fr G
guess what lov-er I'm leav-ing.
guess I'd bet-ter be leav-ing.
I don't wan-na
Am F C Gsus 3fr
be that guy, to look you in the face and lie,

G Gsus2 G Am F
Some-one has to say it first, e-ven if the
To Coda
Dm G Gsus2 G Am F
words may hurt. I on-ly love you,
C G
I on - ly, love you, I on - ly love you, on - ly
Gsus G Am F
3fr
love you, on - ly love you when I'm drunk. I on - ly love you,

C
Gsus
3fr
I on - ly love you,
I on - ly love you, on - ly
G
C
F
love you, on - ly love you when I'm drunk. Don't get me wrong. Last night I
Dm
Gsus
3fr
did - n't change my mind.
It was the drink; it was
G
C
F
Dm
lead - ing me blind.
And when I kissed you, it was such a big mis - take.

Gsus
3fr
G
C
A couple drinks, that's the chance that I take.
F
D.S. al Coda
And if I can't control all of the things I do, I
CODA
C
F
I only love you, I only, love you,
Am7
Gsus
3fr
G
Gsus2
G
I only love you, only love you, only love you when I'm

Am
F
drunk. I on - ly love __ you, __ I on - ly love __ you, __
Dm7
G7sus
G7
I on - ly love you, on - ly love you, on - ly love you when I'm
C
F
drunk. I on - ly love __ you, __ I on - ly love __ you, __
Am7
Gsus
3fr
G
Gsus2
G
I on - ly love you, on - ly love you, on - ly love you when I'm

Am
F
drunk. I on - ly love you, I on - ly love you,
Dm7
G7sus
I on - ly love you, on - ly love you, on - ly love.
And I may be a
Fmaj7
Cmaj7
lit - tle bit drunk but I know what I've got to do,
Fmaj7
'cause when I get a lit - tle more so - ber I know I'll be o - ver you.

G7sus
C
F
And I may be a lit - tle bit drunk but I
Am7
Gsus
G
Gsus2
G
know what I've got to do, 'cause when I get a
Am7
F
lit - tle more so - ber I know I'll be o - ver you.
Dm7
Gsus
I on - ly love you, I on - ly love you,

C
F
I only love you, I only love you,
Am7
Gsus
3fr
G
Gsus2
G
I only love you, only love you, only love you when I'm
Am
F
drunk. I only love you, I only love you,
Dm7
G7sus
N.C.
I only love you, only love you, only love you when I'm drunk.

# STEP WITH ME

Words and Music by MIKA,
HILLARY LINDSEY and MATHIEU JOMPHE

Moderately fast
Eb 3fr
Ab 4fr
Eb 3fr
mf
Bb
Eb 3fr
Ab 4fr
Is this hap - pen - ing to me?
Eb 3fr
Bb
Have I lost all my dif - f'ren - ces?
Eb 3fr
Ab 4fr
Eb 3fr
Should I wait a - round and see
what it's like to lose my

B♭
E♭
3fr
A♭
4fr
sens - es? Al - ways look - ing for the chance
E♭
3fr
B♭
from the hot girl to the beach - es.
E♭
3fr
A♭
4fr
E♭
3fr
But the chase I'll nev - er miss; now I know what hap - pi -
B♭
E♭
3fr
B♭
ness is. This love's de - li - cious, like

Eb
Ab
Cm
home - cooked dish - es I taste them
Fm
Bbsus
Bb
mis - chiev - ous - ly.
Eb
Ab
Eb
Step one: come a lit - tle clos - er. Step two: rest
Bb
Eb
Ab
up - on my shoul - der. Step three: I'm call - ing you, ba - by, three
3fr
4fr

Cm
B♭
E♭
3fr
steps a - way from me. (Three steps, three steps.) Step four: we
A♭
4fr
E♭
B♭
can get mar - ried. Step five: tak - ing in the cher - ry.
E♭
A♭
Step six: as good as you kiss. Now come
To Coda
Cm
B♭
E♭
a - long and step with me. (Three steps, three steps.)

A♭
Cm
B♭
E♭
A♭
E♭
Sun is shin - ing up a - head.
In thir - ty years we'll still be
B♭
E♭
A♭
hap - py,
mak - ing mov - ies in my head,
E♭
B♭
mak - ing Hol - ly - wood look ti - ny.

E♭
A♭
Don't know why, but all your words
E♭
B♭
E♭
sound just like a mel - o - dy.
From the piec - es that I've
A♭
E♭
B♭
D.S. al Coda
heard, I can build a sym - pho - ny. This
CODA
E♭
A♭
steps.) Step one: I don't e - ven know ya.
8va

E♭ 3fr
B♭
E♭ 3fr
Step two: come a lit - tle clos - er. Step three: you
(8va)
A♭ 4fr
Cm/G 3fr
B♭/F
B♭
can't e - ven see you're three steps from lov - ing me.
(8va)
E♭ 3fr
A♭ 4fr
E♭ 3fr
steps.) Step one: come a lit - tle clos - er. Step two: rest
B♭
E♭ 3fr
A♭ 4fr
up - on my shoul - der. Step three: I'm call - ing you ba - by, three

Cm
B♭
E♭
steps a - way from me. (Three steps, three steps.) Step four: we
A♭
E♭
B♭
can get mar - ried. Step five: tak - ing in the cher - ry.
E♭
A♭
Step six: as good as it gets. Now come
Cm
B♭
E♭
a - long and step with me. (Three steps, three steps.)

# POPULAR SONG

Words and Music by MIKA,
STEPHEN SCHWARTZ, PRISCILLA RENEA
and MATHIEU JOMPHE

Moderately slow
E♭ B♭ A♭ E♭ B♭
mf
A♭ E♭ B♭/E♭
1, 2
A♭/E♭ E♭
Rap I: (See additional lyrics)
3
A♭/E♭ E♭ B♭/E♭
(Rap ends) Mm? Ah. Oh, said I'm
A♭/E♭ E♭ B♭/E♭
put-ting down my sto-ry in a pop-u-lar song. My prob - lem: I nev-er was a

A♭/E♭ E♭ B♭/E♭
3fr
mod - el; I nev - er was a schol - ar, but you were al - ways
A♭/E♭ E♭ B♭/E♭
3fr
pop - u - lar. You were sing - ing all the songs I
A♭/E♭ E♭ B♭/E♭
3fr
don't know. Now you're in the front row, 'cause my song is
A♭ E♭ B♭
4fr 3fr
pop - u - lar. Pop - u - lar. I know about

A♭
E♭
B♭
pop - u - lar. It's not a - bout who you are or your fan - cy car; you're
on - ly ev - er who you were. Pop - u - lar. Who cares a - bout
pop - u - lar? And all that you need to do is be true to you, that's
all you ev - er need to know. Catch up, 'cause you got an aw - ful long way to go.

A♭
E♭
B♭
To Coda
Catch up, 'cause you got an aw - ful long way to go.
A♭
E♭/G
Fm
E♭
B♭/E♭
Rap II: (See additional lyrics)
8vb
1-3
A♭/E♭
E♭
4
A♭/E♭
E♭
B♭/E♭
A♭/E♭
E♭
B♭/E♭
A♭/E♭
E♭
D.S. al Coda
(Rap ends) My

CODA
A♭ E♭/G Fm E♭
B♭
Rap III: (See additional lyrics)
8vb
1 A♭ E♭
2 A♭ E♭
(Rap ends) All you ev - er need to know:
B♭ A♭ E♭
you're on - ly ev - er who you were. All you ev - er need to know:
B♭ A♭ E♭
you're on - ly ev - er who you were. All you ev - er need to know.

B♭
A♭
4fr
E♭
3fr
Pop - u - lar. I know_ a - bout pop - u - lar. It's not_ a - bout
(All you ev - er need to know.)_
B♭
A♭
4fr
E♭
3fr
who you are or your fan - cy car; you're on - ly ev - er who you were._
(All you ev - er need to know.)_
B♭
A♭
4fr
E♭
3fr
Pop - u - lar. I know_ a - bout pop - u - lar, and all_ that you
(All you ev - er need to know.)_
B♭
A♭
4fr
E♭
3fr
need to do is be true to you. That's all you ev - er need to know._
All you ev - er need to know:_

B♭
A♭
4fr
E♭
3fr
you're on - ly ev - er who you were.
All you ev - er need to know:
B♭
1
A♭
4fr
E♭
3fr
you're on - ly ev - er who you were.
All you ev - er need to know.
2
A♭
4fr
E♭
3fr
All you ev - er need to know.


*Rap Lyrics*

*Rap I:*

You were the popular one, the popular chick.
It is what it is. Now I'm popular, bitch.
Standing on the field with your pretty pom-pom,
Now you're working at the movies, selling popular corn.
I could've been a mess, but I never went wrong,
'Cause I'm putting down my stories in a popular song.

*Rap II:*

Always on the lookout for someone to hate,
Pickin' on me like a dinner plate.
I hid during classes and in between them.
Dunk me in the toilets; now it's you that cleans them.
Trying to make me feel bad with the shit you do.
It ain't so funny when the joke's on you.
Ooh! The joke's on you, and everyone's
Laughing, got everyone clapping, asking,
"How come you look so cool?"
Well, that's the only thing that I learned at school.
What? Uh huh. Hmm? See, that's the
Only thing that I learned at school.

*Rap III:*

Before the next time that you call him crazy,
Lazy, a faggot, or that fugayzee,
Here's the one thing that's so amazing:
It ain't a bad thing to be a loser, baby.

# EMILY

Words and Music by MIKA,
JODI MARR and LAURENT LESCARRET

Moderately fast
B♭
F
E♭
B♭/D
Em - i - ly.
Em - i - ly.
f
B♭/F
B♭
F
Gm
F
B♭
Em - i - ly, can't you write a hap - py
E♭
song, can't you ask a num - ber one? You could try a lit - tle

F Eb/G Bb/F Bb
hard - er. Em - i - ly, you could be a mil - lion -
F/Bb Eb/Bb Bb F/Bb Gm/Bb F/Bb
aire, but you're so full of hot air, gon - na end up like your fa - ther. Em - i -
Bb F Eb Bb/D
ly, you can be the luck - y champ - ion. Get a boy and learn to
ly, are you stuck up? Are you gay? If you are, well, that's o -
Bb
dance, be a girl like an - y
kay, 'cause it does - n't e - ven
1 F Eb Bb/D
oth - er. Em - i -
2 F Eb Bb/D
mat - ter. Em - i - ly.

B♭
F
Em - i - ly, it's your life and you can't live it twice.
Gm
E♭maj7/G
E♭maj7
E♭6
3fr
One day you'll un - der - stand. Em - i - ly, take my hand.
B♭
F
Em - i - ly, I love you and I know you do too.
E♭maj7/G
E♭
3fr
You nev - er make no sense, scream - ing at me in French.

B♭ F E♭ B♭/D
3fr
Pour - quoi tu gâches ta vie? Pour - quoi tu gâches ta vie?
To Coda
B♭ F E♭ B♭/D
3fr
Em - i - ly.
Shut up; lis - ten to me. Dance with me, Em - i - ly.
B♭ F E♭ B♭/D
3fr
Pour - quoi tu gâches ta vie? Pour - quoi tu gâches ta vie?
B♭ F E♭ B♭/D
3fr
Em - i -
Shut up; lis - ten to me. Dance with me, Em - i - ly.

B♭ F E♭ B♭/D
ly, you've got so much in your life; me, I've got no one's ad -
B♭ F E♭/G B♭/F
vice. Don't you know you've got it eas - y? Em - i -
B♭ F E♭ B♭/D
ly, what you smok - in'? What's that stench? Who you scream - in' at in
B♭ F E♭ B♭/D
French? Did you real - ly think you had me? Em - i -

B♭
F
E♭
B♭/D
ly, that's e - nough to have you chose, act - ing like you're eight years
B♭
F
E♭
B♭/D
old. I give up; it's not worth try - in'. Em - i -
B♭
F
E♭
B♭/D
Gm
ly, one day I will end up dead; that's the on - ly thing I've said that will ev - er get her
F
E♭
B♭/D
D.S. al Coda
smil - ing. Em - i - ly.
CODA
B♭
Pour - quoi tu gâches ta vie?

F
E♭
3fr
B♭/D
B♭
Em - i - ly.
Pour - quoi tu gâches ta vie? Shut up; lis - ten to me:
F
E♭
3fr
B♭/D
B♭
Em - i - ly, leave your life in a bal -
dance with me, Em - i - ly.
F
E♭/B♭
6fr
Dm/B♭
B♭
loon, lock your - self up in a room so the world can nev - er
F/A
E♭/G
3fr
B♭/F
E♭maj7
3fr
reach you. Em - i - ly, and I'm speak - ing Jap - a -

F Eb/F Dm/F Gm
nese. Got me fall - ing on my knees; got me pray - ing to Saint
F/A Eb/G Bb/F Bb
Pe - ter. Em - i - ly, you see the price I had to
F Eb/Bb Dm/Bb Bb
pay. I would give my life a - way if I knew that I could
F/A Eb/G Bb/F Ebmaj7
reach her. Em - i - ly, why'd you make this hard for
8vb

F
E♭/F
Dm/F
Gm
F/A
E♭/B♭
me? It's not the way it's meant to be. I don't ev - er wan - na hate you. Em - i - ly,
(8vb)
B♭
F
Gm
dance. Em - i - ly, dance, dance, dance. Em - i - ly, dance. Em - i - ly,
E♭
B♭
dance, dance, dance. Em - i - ly, dance. Em - i - ly,
F
Gm
E♭maj7/G
(Em - i - ly. _
dance, dance, dance. Em - i - ly, dance, dance, dance, dance, dance, dance, dance. Em - i - ly,

B♭
F
Em - i - ly,
dance. Em - i - ly, it's your life and you can't live it twice.
Gm
E♭maj7/G
E♭maj7
E♭6
3fr
yeah.) (Em - i - ly.
One day you'll un - der - stand. Em - i - ly, take my hand.
B♭
F
Em - i - ly,
Em - i - ly, I love you and I know you do too.
E♭maj7/G
E♭maj7
E♭6
3fr
yeah.) (Em - i - ly.
You nev - er make no sense, scream - ing at me in French.

Bb
F
Eb
Bb/D
Em - i - ly.)
Pour - quoi tu gâches ta vie? Pour - quoi tu gâches ta vie?
(Em - i - ly.
Shut up; lis - ten to me. Dance with me, Em - i - ly.
Em - i - ly.)
Pour - quoi tu gâches ta vie? Pour - quoi tu gâches ta vie?
Em - i - ly, dance.
Shut up; lis - ten to me. Dance with me, Em - i - ly.

# HEROES

Words and Music by MIKA,
OLI CHANG, NICHOLAS LITTLEMORE
and JACK MILAS

Moderately fast
A5
mp
The kids in the hun - dreds, to -
E5
F♯m
mor - row will march through the door.
They're
D5
A5
fight - ing some - one else - 's war.
They'll have

E5
F♯m
so man - y sto - ries to tell in ex -
D5
5fr
A
change for a he - ro's fare - well. I wish I could, I
E/G♯
F♯m
wish I could make you re - turn. And
D
A
E/G♯
what if I'll nev - er dis - cern as you walk to the toll of the

F♯m
D
A
bell, you'll be fight - ing for our heav - en with hell. And
E
F♯m
D
It's your
you don't un - der - stand why no one else can see your
A
E
F♯m7
blood on me, and my blood on you;
D
A
E
but to make you bleed, the on - ly thing I

F♯m7
1
D
would - n't do.
A
E
And you know, he - roes aren't meant to sur - vive.
F♯m7
D(add2)
A
So much hard - er to love when a - live.
E
F♯m7
Walk with the dev - il in your head.
You wouldn't

D(add2)
A
think you were bet-ter off dead. And
2, 3
D
A
E/G♯
Where can you go?
Where can you
Fight-in', fight-in', fight-in'.
(We can't go far.)
F♯m7
D(add2)
A/E
go?
Fight-in', fight-in', fight-in'.
We fight, we earn, we nev-
E
F♯m7
To Coda
-er learn, and through it all, the he-

D
A(add2)
D(add2)
-ro falls.
I wish there was a way
E(add4)
A
to give you a hand to hold,
A(add2)
D
E(add4)
F♯m
'cause you don't have to die in
D
A
E
glo - ry,
die to nev - er grow

A
A/E
old. It's your blood on me,
E
F♯m
D
and my blood on you; but to
A
E
F♯m
make you bleed, the on-ly thing I would-n't do.
D
D.S. al Coda
(take 3rd ending)
It's your
CODA
D
A
-ro falls.

# CELEBRATE

Words and Music by MIKA,
BENJAMIN JAMES HENRY JACK GARRETT
and PHARRELL WILLIAMS

Moderately fast
D7sus
(I want the whole world to cel - e - brate.)
f
C
Dsus
G
Bm/A
C
Dsus
G
Bm/A
C
Dsus
G
Bm/A
I wan - na come home to the on - ly

C Dsus G Bm/A
place I know, where the trees are
fin - ish line. Does - n't mat - ter if I
C Dsus G Bm/A C Dsus
plant - ed, grow. I wan - na come home.
take my time. I'm com - ing home.
G Bm/A C D(add4)
Once I get up, I feel bet -
G Am13 C D(add4)
- ter and I pull my - self to - geth - er. I re - mem - ber those two let -
3fr

G
Am13
C
D(add4)
3fr
- ters; it will be O K. Ev - 'ry - one says now or nev -
G
Am13
C
D(add4)
3fr
- er; I say on - ly if it's bet - ter. Be - ing young like this for - ev -
G
Am13
Cmaj7
D(add4)
3fr
G(add2)
- er, but we know bet - ter. I want the whole world to cel - e - brate.
Cmaj7
D(add4)
3fr
G(add2)
I want the whole world to cel - e - brate.

Cmaj7
D(add4)
G(add2)
3fr
I want the whole world to cel - e - brate.
1
Cmaj7
D(add4)
G(add2)
C
Dsus
I want the whole world to cel - e - brate.
I'll be just fine
G
Bm/A
when I see you at the
2
Cmaj7
D(add4)
G(add2)/D
I want the whole world to cel - e - brate.
Am7
Dsus
(Spoken:) I'm not mad at you at all, but,
(Sung:) I want the

G(add2)
whole world to cel - e - brate.
Cmaj7
C(add2)
G/B
Am7
G/B
(Spoken:) Right about now it's time for everybody to stand up
(Sung:) and have
C(add2)
G/B
Am11
3fr
fun, 'cause we've just be - gun. I want the

Dsus
C(add2)
whole world to cel - e - brate. Once I get up, I feel bet -
G/B
Am11
3fr
- ter and I pull my - self to - geth - er. I re - mem - ber those two let -
G/B
G7/B
C(add2)
- ters; it will be O - K. Ev - 'ry - one says now or nev -
G/B
Am11
3fr
- er; I say on - ly if it's bet - ter. Be - ing young like this for - ev -

Dsus
C
D(add4)
G
Bm/A
3fr
I wan-na come home.
I wan-na come home.
(I want the whole world to cel - e - brate.)
- er. (I'm com - ing home.)
(I'm com - ing
C
D(add4)
G
Bm/A
C
D(add4)
I wan-na come home.
(I want the whole world to cel - e - brate.)
(I want the
home.)
(I'm com - ing home.)
G
Bm/A
C
D(add4)
G
Bm/A
I wan-na come home
to cel - e - brate.
whole world to cel - e - brate.)
(I want the whole world to cel - e - brate.)
(I'm com - ing home.)
(I'm com - ing

C D(add4) G Bm/A C D(add4)
I'll get the whole world to cel - e - brate. I want the
(I'm com - ing home.)
home.)
G Bm/A C D(add4)
whole world to cel - e - brate.
(I want the
(I'm com - ing home.)
G Bm/A C G5
whole world to cel - e - brate.)
(I'm com - ing home.)